Psalmandala

Poems By
Michael Patrick Collins

ELJ Publications ~ New York

ELJ Editions

ISBN-13: 978-942004-06-6

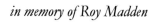

in memory of Roy Madden

CONTENTS

III

IV

ACKNOWLEDGEMENTS

Grateful acknowledgment is made to the following journals in which these poems originally appeared—perhaps in a slightly different form: *BlazeVOX, Blood Lotus Journal, The Broken City, Constellations: A Journal of Poetry and Fiction, Danse Macabre, Dressing Room Poetry Journal, Eunoia Review, Ginosko Literary Journal, Glasschord Art and Culture Magazine, Grist Journal, Inclement Poetry Magazine, Kenning Journal, Mobius: The Journal of Social Change, The Pennwood Review, PressBoardPress Magazine, Red Paint Hill Quarterly, Riverbabble, Slippery Elm Literary Journal, Smartish Place, SOFTBLOW, Stoneboat Literary Journal, Subliminal Interiors Literary Arts Magazine,* and *The Subterranean Quarterly.*

Nightmare with Reader

The devil painted a picture

of a monster
eating a child.

The monster looked just like you.

In his way the devil is honest:

You really are
a monster sometimes.

The child looked just like you too.

As if you could only be one

or the other.
Nothing else.

He says *choose*. He is also an angel.

With dark magic he made the ground

of the painting
reflect light.

See. It looks just like a mirror.

I

Metamorphosis

Upon waking Facebook informs me
my account's been suspended due to suspicion
that I'm not an actual person,

and I want to make this travesty of reason
into a poem about how the interwebs
are the new underworld and this brazen theft

of my personhood is a symbolic death
by isolation – no, a punishment,
lived out in the internetartarus,

perpetrated by the invisible lords of creation,
so I try combing *The Metamorphoses*,
for some edgy mythical references,

but it's so much with the death and rape
and people becoming trees and animals,
it occurs to me if it got turned

into a movie it'd be a snuff porn.
I wander out onto the porch to console myself,
trying to create an image of importance

by pacing and pausing with my cigarette,
and then that two-year-old appears
in the neighbor's window, waiting for me

once again to become Sir Fantastic
of the Magic Ballooning Cheeks
that helium me up on tiptoes,

my fingers now pins bursting the illusion,
leaving me flying down onto the deck,
disinflated and rich with the child's laughter,

sharp and audible through the pane, and
my soul awakens, begins to imagine me
through pictures of children who might still incarnate:

this one the architect of the Lincoln Log
megalopolis that spans a bedroom;
this one sings garland onto the Tree;

this one, who dives, flying-squirrel-like
from trampolines, known far and wide for braving
the ropeswing and hollering *kersplosh*

in the still chilled water of just new June;
this one, who learns bird calls and sneaks in strays,
makes small graves for roadkill, and dies too young –

while the real boy is pounding his window,
loudly, screeching cacophonous encores,
not for a second thinking my trance

was anything more than a part of our game,
already poking his own swollen face
with tiny fingers in preemptive mimesis,

clapping hysterically at his exploding cheeks,
delighted beyond reason in this moment,
this innocent glimpse into how quickly

he can be taken by whim and transformed.

My Soul Delivers a Eulogy for My Grandfather

"As in ancient stories, when deaths of kings
obliged some enerdreadful hero
with armor dyed in brigands' blood
to capture weeping eyes with valor,
give all the freedom to pray for the king's soul
and not for mercy,
                so you imagine
you must take your tears and rageful shaking
for the life Time has sentenced to memory
to the taleold forge behind your heart,
where your anger forms pain into calling,
death into hell's salivating hounds,
yourself into village fathers mustered,
clutching, deathwilling, to axes and shovels
to stand between wickedness and their children–
A fantasy? Yes, but at least it grants you
an enemy you can pretend to defeat,
so your psyche again can return
to the everealm in which it once rehearsed
the stories he watched you play into the world,
as if,   by retreating in time, you'd defeat it –

Then baptize your sweord edge with villainblood;
scatter imaginevil carcasses;
return exhausted, intrepid, your own death
forgotten again so that you might delusion
you'll somehow sleep without awakening
                    to mourning
for one who made it safe to placreate
with his giant's grin, his thundering,
"Well, I think you must be onto something,"
when you performed one of your nonsense stories

of Klingon wars or the secret tree folk,
nurturing portals with his audiessence,
through which you could journey into the middleworld
as he lawnchaired and stillwatched on autumn evenings
while you saved Gondor from the orkish hordes,
won a thirty or forty World Series,   transformed
the enormous Oak by the road into Endor,
and learned to speak with deer and cardinals –

He gave you our liminal space still within you,
where I wait yet, echoing: *He didn't leave you;*
he left me   to listen until you say *thank you*
for reknowing his soulhoming even today
in the worldmaking pagevoices of ancients,
then in a softer murmur of creek, a whisper
of breeze through the pine trees above the small children
you'll watch running playcrazy shouting like Banshees,
ecstatic at routing their improvised rogues,
inhaling your silence to shout forth the hidden,
invisible worlds through which the quick ghosts
of those who have loved you smuggle their laughter
through bars of birdsong, their gracious smiles
onto strangers in restaurants and old men
with ridiculous, gigantic plastic
fingers, singing with their delighted
grandchildren at ballgames, their patient wrinkles
onto the newancient wintermind faces
of young men who still stand, facing graves."

Soul's Parable

"This is not the breeze that held the twelve villagers together, or the crows who squawked, guarding the forest to the west. Those gathered are not standing in a circle. There is no hawk on the horizon, no woman with subtle wrinkles below her eyes with her hair in a bun who will not submit to tears, nor any such thing as a small girl delighting a haze of rose petals around the couple in the center. This is not the small bag packed and waiting behind the table at his mother's, but only the ring he offered the finger of the last girl he would kiss. It was springtime. The year that the war came."

My Soul Apocalypses My Dream

"The dream the poem rebirths is not the dream.
The dream the poem destroys is not the dream.

What matter if I myth around what was?
That the gods had rained down flames upon the earth,

transfigured landscape into memory,
as if the constellations had demanded

to be reunited with the mortal mythwives,
through whom they were born, for whom they carried

unspeakable pain to their fablegraves.
Small bands of livedons left to starve and salvage.

Knew they must journey to lands unseen
to build a new world for their children.

Yet they feared, for the youngest was sick,
would never survive the privations of travel.

Yet they feared that the gods they had angered
would not allow passage without a sacrifice.

So the leader, whose leg the blitheyed dancer loved
to cling to, circled his people around the child.

Commanded he dance, said it was medicine –
the boy whose grin reflected the quickshadow

of the soul to whom the old man had grown strifeblind
as she suffocated under his sworn duty,

though he would never let it be spoken,
though he would never relinquish the ghost

of the spiraling, childancing tike, his arms
a tornado, one leg then the other

earthquaking painlessly for their amusement,
his hair alighting as the ducks once had

when couples strolled too close for comfort
by their perches near the esplanade,

his tongue wagging like a young sheepdog,
his teeth still shining despite the misery,

as if he would dance forever.
                   And then,
the old man closed his eyes and made a fist.

And the circle they had to preserve kicked the child to death.
Life given to the invisible that life continue,

for every apocalypse is a negation,
for every apocalypse is an expression.

And all you can firemind *is how horrifying!*
Yes, they will summon a legend from their dead world

of a childgod who gave himself for his tribe,
freely and willingly loving himself toward the torture;

they will lifesong a worldmother who, in her kind-
vicious vision, claims every beloved existence

that temporal affection would permit
to stifle the wholife; then finally a fathersky

whose creations so pained and betrayed him
with their ingratitude and malice,

he had to incinerate their wickedness;
he had to let the survivorighteous inherit –

Have you not also put to death what couldn't live?
Endlessed what never could be spoken

in mattertime into an epic? You *realize*:
What for them was ceremony in you poems.

For songlone fleshlings live by lyricing such dreams
into your shamed and sacremaciated world,

dreams in which the slaughturial dignifies
the necessevil, permits timelings

to render myths of loves that only bones will suffer,
to bury them between the lines that bind the brilliant stars."

To a Thief

You know what you did, you sociopathic jackwagon. And don't
think I don't know a poem can't recover what's been stolen. This is
just to say I've learned that thinking of you only makes me another
sniveling citizen of your psychotic little kleptocracy. So you made
me feel like I had no home. Great, go post it on Crookbook. Today
I remembered when I was a child, driving home one night with my
mom and grandparents. In northern Michigan we always played a
game of who could spot the deer first. If you hit one with your car,
you'll probably die, so it was kind of a wise game to play. That
night, my grandpa yelled, *Well, there's one, Michael,* but then on
reflection, retracted: *Oh, hell, never mind, that's a house,* and we
laughed like his body would never be ashes. This is just to say we
are still laughing in that remembrance, in that Cadillac I'll never ride
in again, in that memory you will never take away.

Underworld

As my drowsy apartment becomes outer darkness,
I move through the thick dew toward the train,
and fast as a sleight of hand the Guidethief
waves his snakestaff, mercurys breezes
that wake the evermores inside me
who lie beneath the worksmile and whatiflines
under my eyes, beyond maybesomeday,
past every eyeveil of my blooded suffering,
and the sound of my footsteps seems the meter
of this lyricworld I once again traverse
as my eyes hermeneutic the streetlights
that slice through the darkness and now seem to carve
a clear path forward, each one whispering
its riddle to me through the fog,
and I feel myself clothed –   or swallowed? –
in that blanketish chamomile feeling that follows,
knowing the kindawful chthon of souls
that we *daily* strive to enlighten away
now surrounds me in calmtearful knowledge –
As if, in this deathsight, all that once was quick
reveals its hidden, foreverimage:
Memory awakens into metaphor
as two worlds see that they are one,
startle   one another awake with their presence,

and I don't know why the guide of my soul
has always uncompromised me forward
since my first bodyhome in onceonly time,
where I shivered unseens in the silence,
iceveined *all* the night might have been hiding.
The city that circled me a sleeping hell.
Where criminals wished to hubris into gods.

For pride was the homicide of meaning.
Strength the mad cackle that echoes despair.
The desire to burn one's soul   to light the world –
The god of thieves gotawayed and fasthanded,
bound by no loyalty to Iamhes
who illusioned themselves in his image.
Like the first kid to break into our house.
Who then got shot and set on fire.
By the same guys who'd mugged my friend
and me in the park the year before.
A cop we knew told us –   *true story.*
He chuckled.   Like this made the universe moral.
And three wrongs make a right was the new two.
And we all laughed. As if the capricious
eventual could be confined
in gossip and newscasts and nightmares….

Which makes it seem as if this is a story
about what was stolen   not what I learned
the night I was home alone down in the basement,
where I built cities filled with citizens
who arrowscorned and valorspeared my epics,
the fear I disowned recreated in play
as my children rehearsed all the murder around me,
my silence the architect of a scream –
Heard something. Fear assumed *burglar.*
Grabbed the knife left resting on the plate
from dinner. Lurked next to the door.
Ready to ram it through this intruder's throat.
Turned out the light. Let my eyes readjust.
To the darkness. The only certain –
Protect me tearblood furious ready.
                              Come.

Fear and lost anger had finally awakened
someone who was ready to fight for his life.
How kind is the god who has brought me
to this other death, this home of souleye,
who sees past the killer who lives in my mind,
from whom I huddled in murderous terror,
into the image that now ends the story
each time the memory immortals inside me:
the knifebloodless, darkendless emptiness
I saw when I first opened the door,
full of no one to love or destroy me –
and then nothing   beyond it but the tips
of the newstrange stairs leading upward.

Kenosis

The night I knew I was *never* going to sleep with Natalie Portman,
never win *either* the World Cup or Pulitzer, speak in tongues, in
revelations, prophesies and daggers, be adored by the whole of
creation, held by arms that would stay there forever, I knew that I
would be the servant, one day beaten, the next invisible, a ghost
begging breezes for tastes of pineapple, a touch of cashmere, smell
of lavender, the world one giant lidded eye and I a fallen lash
because I knew it was one or the other, idol or beggar, whip or skin
flayed worshipful – I knew there was only one escape, but instead I
went out for a walk, alongside the rows of houses I was locked out
of, and the angel who had released me from every fantasy that had
barred him lifted my head to souleye the lights starring towards me.

II

My Soul's Self-Portrait

"Listen to how her hair whistles   the way a small girl does
when she first learns, how   the gentle curls howl

like circling wolves. The smile   tastes like the salt-
laced wind by the bay,   eyes that feel

like the first blanket you ever were   wrapped in, the first fist
that left a mark. You want me   to draw the body, but it's

the eyes with their centers of mid-   night, dark as
the future, patient   as death, as ghosts. They taste

like mangos. They drip   down your forehead like
a dream. You are rolling down   a grass hill in fresh dew. You are

a monk, a whore, a troubadour,   a widower. She is
your citadel, your onlylove, your other   name, the sand of the lake

you swam at the dawn of   memory. She will never relinquish
your vision; you'll never forgive   the actual girl for not being

the being   you saw."

Good Friday

Today's truth cries not   from the mothercalm quiet
of the cave, nor the springust bird-

                     song
of ascent, but in nails and splinters of souleyed pain,

ribs splitting in slowicked

                     increments,
the tickle of blood trickling down the brow,
and vinegar, *yes*,   it tastes better

than this metallic abandonment, *yes*,
vinegar vinegar, all   that will ever
be left – The death of a god

             is known

inside you, shorn   of those loved
with whom he mortaled, a voice that knows
the wages of being

          rendered.

Yet earth and rock are still   my home:
As I hear the anguish of the murdered

               son,
back into the corpseworld, my own soul asks

how long she must hang

            unseen here in my shadows,
how long before I will sing   her back
into a creation that childs and holds me,

back into the birds and trees and caves and tyrants,

and what to the terrified eye

                              appear

to be indifferent hills   of stone?

Yantranelle

When the terraciting voice

                  of soul is *known*,

dissignification ones us

                in vaporapture,

unforming mindfire constructions with glee-   vil dreamtones,
for each language is hers that is not y-   ours, owned —
Listengo! The othertongues open soul-   ventures

when the terraciting voice of

                      soul is

                            known:

Semantics cedes

              all dayphrases

                       to dreamnotes;

each emanation death-

              homes

                    to its center,

unforming mindfire con-

                structions with gleevil dream-

                          tones:

Each drop offers itself   .   The soulocean wholes.

Though earth-

           vision ice-

                veins, monotones, dismembers.

When the terra-

             citing voice of

                    soul is *known*.

Glut-

      orders lesspokens colonized to song-

                        bones.

For each mystery-

          tongue heartdrums name-

                     less disorder.

Unforming mind-   fire constructions with gleevil dreamtones.
Oceaneye! The griefthroes of the World-   's Soul!
You'll, like the matterowns! Wish her   a metaphor!

When

      the terraciting voice of soul is known.
Un-

      forming mindfire constructions with gleevil dreamtones.

Portrait of my Soul in Trees

Outside our apartment
                           trees stormed with the twister
as rainclaws mauled bricks and squalls assaulted glasswalls,
branchlimbs   reveling together in one ocean,

leafeet keeping meter, time   becoming allgreen,
onesouled in the knowing that everflow alwaysed,
spirit glimpsed in wind, portrait
                                danced into image;

a family of old trees
                      who someone had Rockwelled
down by the harbor to shade the paths and benches
where blissful picnicks picturesqued,   kids childed.

Meanwhile ripped from their
                                 earth by the same wild spirals.
Now lay in a row like execution victims.
Roots still clench stones like teddy bears   neweyes quicksight

into inspi-
           ration. Holes gaping below them –
The image my soul's graveway from brushing pictures
of herself through eyes   of this corpseworld she adores

to lonely whol-
               laging of fragments in deathsight,
unsplintering all contræmotions back to circle.
Accepting all life. Living only   by witness.

Unseen. Eternity mourns no mort-
                                life. Envies.

Psalmandala

When I firesight
        the first   word,
                  the silenspace be-   tween us
   demises   me under a pyrocidal
             flood
until   I can't imagine
           where rod and staff
could possibly linger   with their comfort,
and I want
     to ask what   is the purpose
of a god
    damn shepherd that leaves me   deflocked,

    except in my terror-
         eyes the   psalm
has already mindivided:
         reference
             to monster,
patrolling the depths   all these thousands
             of years,
all the ocean   its table – devours   me
            whole:
  I flamebeg the cruel-   mighty lamb of the holy-
            sword,
  breathcandle the death-
     judge of   book and time- scythe
to make a down pay-
     ment on eye-
        foraneye,
and my soul remembers
     the Leviathacidal dread- knife

that formed

the heavens   from its horror,

for I re-

call   that you are myth-

figured

through   soul   -   eye's   sickwise visions,

for I have   forgotten that I-

am a fraction,

that, in this shadow-   valley in which I life-

psalm,

the Azraeline specters

who seem to threaten me

are merely visions   of my silencend,

demanding I death-

sentence to your world, Lord   of Ends,

where one

are the staff   and the sword,

for when my corpse-

voice has rendered

the darkness

to portraitext, I icevein

darkness no longer,

for it too is Yours; in these finalines   you hold me,

my Valley,

my Shadow,

my Cupoverflowing,

O Soul-

                 pasture dew-   greening morningly
toward

                 my completion,   creator
          from creator   to creator,
yea, though this picture-

                              song of the always
here-

          now   holds and lullabys you,
swaddled

                 in saccrilines, this moment   's everchild.

Post-Modern, Post-Secular Apology

In retrospect, I *might-*   shouldnta mentioned
to the guy who came
        seveneight "boyfriends" later

that you had the clap. I wasn't really   *that* mad
you were having so much
        more sex than me.

Or even that I was   too troubadubescent
to listen
      when friends would testify.

Truth is I loved the way you rendered   all
with your nihilomantic mind-
      scythe.

Then later performed your *don'tleaveme-*
      this*way.*
Cast me as "faithful." Too stoned to see-*right*through a window.

I wasn't even that taken   aback
when you laughed and spit vodka the night
      I professed,

"I love you." *Some*part-
      ofme knew
I really was   *that* ridiculous.

You were, too. Just   never at the same time.
Chased each other
      inandout of desperation.

Two planets hell-

                  bent on conquering the sun
in their *begone-*   *complete*me cycling.

Really,   *who* would have *ever* loved *either* of us?
Worldmangling creators! Intrepitwit art-

                            ists!

Creators of nonsense

               conglomerations
and fragments. Too jaded and pre-   scient

for the "cliché"   that we'd "whole" one another,
each guided by the trans-

                    cendental

epiphiwhims of "our

               own" souls. As if
de-   posing the Hallmark™ God, who made

the whole world out of *love*   *'n'bunnies,*
would let us continue on for-

               ever,

pathetic fear-   lings transforming "material"
to avoid our own meta-

               morphoses,

vampiring nightly   from the mirrors
each of our souls showed us in

                  the other –

the belovedread pain we'd *thought*   vanquished, as if

they were teaching us
                    each a lesson,

remaking us *brand*new and moral – or
                                        as if
they themselves wished to be perceived   completely,

not just
                    guides of our insights and visions
but also sick-   wise, also kindviscious.

My Soul's Music Lesson

"You thought you were such a detective
the day you discovered Matilda
was a brand of rum and suddenly

the Tom Waits song about the drunk soldiers
all made sense, how they were so unspeakably
broken and lonely – and she this odd, sole witness

they'd take into their bodies to feel mothered
when all else was endless quickened nightmare.
Alcohol: The case was solved.

Years later I stumbled you across the Aussie
ballad of the World War I vet with legs
blown off who can't understand why they still play

"Waltzing Matilda" at veterans parades,
blanketing citizens in patriotic haze,
when all of the bullets and corpses were for nothing

except rhetoric. I let you identify
with him, imagine your feelings into his body
your fears into amputations, start wondering

what song the soldier was so obsessed with
long enough to launch an investigation.
You really thought you had it cold

when Google informed you that "Waltzing Matilda"
was the most famous song in Australia, the song
of a poacher killed by a policeman. "Matilda"

is the sleeping mat that slides back
and forth across a wandering rover's back,
swaying behind him as if they were dancing.

But you kept on digging, uncovered the real
Matilda, not the bottle that followed Tom Traubert
through his mangled world of phantoms

or the song made to betray the maimed soldier,
not even the rover's devoted pack,
that witness who never leaves, always facing

back at where he's been, always dancing
with him down his path toward whatever end,
the whole outback his bedroom, his home, his dream—

You *knew* then I was the whole mystery;
you *knew* then you've always lived inside me.
But, still, all I want is to sing along.

I can only feel inside your body."

Shards for Sophia

In the dream I am running through rooms of an old house.
I am looking for God; I find a mirror in a frame.
I see nothing but darkness   in the mirror.
God was a sarcastic nihilist back then.

*

Darkness, no figure, no sound, no reflection,
a canvas of glass, the empty pause before a song,
the silence after a song   creates its own world.
I swore to sing the night I saw; I vowed to build an empire of wind.

*

You let me think I'd made the world. Matter existed
for me to shape – and longed to claim me.
I wanted to bury myself   in my own creation.
Instead the phone rang; a friend asked how I'd been.

*

During my tryst with belief and religion, a light appeared
in the mirror. Which I feigned into revelation.
The light wed the shadow that held it; the mirror was whole.
I knew every single thing complete and forever   once again.

*

In the library I read about Sophia, Wisdom of God,
mother of the Creator, descending into matter.

I souleye out the window as my alarm clock goes off;
when it becomes a car alarm, I am no longer   reading.

*

When I asked for God, you showed me what I could conceive,
a place where I could someday see my soul, divine
and shattered. You showed me yourself; this is my mirror,
created to reflect you. Take it.   Gaze.

*

I watch the ducks squawking and splashing.
I become a thin mirror in which they appear.
I hold the whole world; I am only a gust of summer.
The ducks and the mirror and I all zoë one soul.

III

Ars Sapientia

Between   the lilac and the rose, between   the laurel and
the willow, home   and journey, dream and sunburn, mud
          and moon, ocean   and broken bone, angel and   sculpted
stone, *here*   you free and claim me, dis-   close paradise
          in a Big Mac wrapper, make me   wait infinite
nevers to lay down   my head on a meadow   made of stars
beside tender   Lethe, unchained from my-   self long enough
to create   you, form   you, beget you   as you would
make me. If you were   Adonai, I   would have knelt. If
you were else-   where, I would have sought   you,
forsaken   the lullaby and the anthem,   the ode, the
oration, the whisper,   the spell. If you were really   a girl, I
would hold   you as if you were   dying, looking   through
this world   back to your native land. I would have brushed
          your hair from your face to frame   your eyes, to see out of
them   with you, conceived   you into steel and
concrete,   arrowheads, milk   bottles, and bombs. If you
were a person,   not an eternity, a person,   not a
timelessness, not a god-   image, not just

                              this —   Listen.
I accept all that   is. Just make me   *yours*   for these
moments; I'll draw   your silhouette, give you   shape
and live with-   in it. If you want   my life,   it's time
          for you to take it.

Ravensong

It was already one of those nights.
When I feel like the almighty
is some hybrid homeosociopath.
Who treats myopia with blindness.
Sentences us to endless journeys deathward.
Then I got side swiped by a *stroller*
in the subway as I tried to high step away.
And this was no docile, civilian contraption.
Oh, no: The kind that the germ-phobic trophy wives drive.
Climate controlled. Hermetically sealed.
Safe and hostile as an Abrams tank.
For the tike on the inside anyway.
And she didn't just lightly strike me, either.
She meant to *smite* me. Her own tiny   lightning war.
And *then* she irately screeched, *excuse me,*
which, of course, in New York dialect
is a euphemism for   *you jackass,*
get out of my way, or I'm pasting
your lifeless brains on the god damn train tracks.
And I couldn't devise the right counter-attack.
What psycho fights moms with strollers, right?
Never mind the child likely had shell shock.
So I compromised, telling her *well*   *ok.*
I mean, you did just ask so nicely.
And sliced up the stairs through the unkindness
of persons perched under the awning,
trying to wait out a rainstorm. Impatient,

I wade through them into the deluge,
and, consequently, I'm soon absolutely drenched
and questioning why I subjected myself
to the rain that has swooned through my jacket

and ruined my shoes and that I can imagine
is hazing its way through my backpack,
revisioning each letter on every page
into a pictogram yet untranslated,
and the babble of rain on the pavement
seems like nature's way to make me deathlaugh
my antediluvian consternation
as her hands dance in the waves of rain
that gathers each individual figure,
places them back into one panorama
as othershuns cover their heads like candles,
scurry back   to separate safety of doorways,
and parades of taxis yellowglaze
their way through the streetwaves, the old trees
still reaching centerward down through the concrete
even while greening high toward the blackwhites
and lightningreys of the quicksilvering oceansky
as somewhere, amidst the kaleidoscopes
cast by the lights of cars and streetlamps,
within this landscape painted by its canvas,
a nescient worldling's souleye opens
to witness itself in this picture
in which he lives, shahids it together;
the rainveil breathes itself into his vision.
He stops;   the areyounuts of the umbrellatopped
streams around him like a creek rock;
he's neither washed on in the everflow
nor left to desiccate on the bank,
Sophia's horizon soonbluing inside him,
the tempest rendering him within her image,
a part of the world that he, for a moment,
knows in its bonekiss he also is.

Dear Reader,

I'm asking you to listen; I can't live
anymore in a light world of water cooler
gossip that always seems to turn
six or seven of the same blank face
when I try to imagine the other side
of people like this week's tabloid villain,
who hid in a rest stop bathroom,
patient as a punch line, waiting
for the right moment, late at night,
when a young man came in alone,
material for a tortured joke, told
by stabbing him twenty times, spreading
rouge in circles on his dead face,
and affixing a rubber clown nose
with a warm knife left to hold it —

But, Reader, Ear to the Poor of Spirit,
surely you can picture with me
the way a man is made into a demon:
Conjure the days of his stomach clenching,
waiting for dad to look up from his whisky
when the boy, as was expected, reported
he had finished his chores and was ready
for bed, so that his dad could glance
at his watch and, with a blithe smirk,
pronounce, *Almost. Maybe someday hiccup
you'll be quick enough*, and fumble
with his belt, ask, calm and deadpan,
for his son's assistance with the buckle,
so that he could watch the child cry twice,
first from the indifference, then the beating,
so that the titan might laugh even harder

as he flogged him, mimic the sobbing,
haw-heh, haw-heh, haw-heh, haw-heh,
and, when finished, send him to bed
with a kick in the ass and an invitation:
Come back tomorrow, donkey boy.
We'll do the whole thing all over again.

Dear Reader, Seer of Total Beings,
decipher the hidden pictographs
this father has drawn in his son's tears:
I've made you the image of my weakness.
You are the part of me I despise.
Go make disciples. Perceive his spreading
of this sick gospel beneath all his shouting
obscenities at teachers' questions,
knocking out praised kids' teeth at recess,
and then laughing in his small heart
all the way home to be whipped by his father
for once as punishment rather than dalliance,
finally master of the twisted snickers
by which he was crafted and knew himself.

Surely You, who never turn Your face,
can imagine the hidden hieroglyphics
the killer's knife didn't know it would leave
upon the body of his subject:
This one is you feeding the dog my dinner;
this one is kids calling me Navajo
when my bruises looked like war paint;
this one's the night when I stopped crying;
the smell of your laughter; the nights your demons
tore my fallen nestling's body
like a stray's teeth with their terrors;

this one's for the violent smile
I wore to make the world make sense,
the one no officer or cell could make me
wipe off of my face, and this —

Dear Reader, O Glorious Impossible,
what if the last one was for a firefly
one of his teachers helped him capture
and watch flicker and wait and flicker,
and she said, *I think he likes you, look*
at all those lights, let him take it home,
but told him tomorrow to let it go,
as if she knew that he would hide it
under his bed, his first real treasure,
until days later, the clicking against glass
ceased in silence, and in his despair
he heard an *I told you so* and laughter
that throbbed like a paper cut with no band-aid?
Or could he have watched it suffer
and for seconds nearly learned to love
through mourning — scared of this peculiar feeling,
returned to cackling, plucking wings,
a life of mocking the brittle objects
he'd learned to make of other people,
each time so certain, for those only moments
in which he felt even caricatures
of the tyrannous contentment
his world had tutored him to covet,
that, he, the stronger, would live on —

Nights when my gravity scoffs at sleep,
my mind too creates another world,

in which such a weedy, pathetic creature
is all I will ever be to you, Reader.

What if that's all he really is to me?

Wisdom,

I must ask: Where   was the father   of that small boy
circled   on that street corner   with his older brother   and
his friends;   was he created

to stretch out his arms   as the elder did   the same,
mirroring him   to trick him   into trusting, forming
him   within a hug, picking him up

and spinning him round and   round, the younger one
glee-   shrieking in the beginning,   one   with this impossible
loving bigness –   but then *still* spinning, betrayed

by that larger   power   he adored, dizzy,   his mind a
cyclone, well   after he was petrified, lost   in tears,   the
worldly friends' cackling   at his nescient vertigapostacy,

set back   on concrete, still   sobbing wildly,   wobbly,
the world vanished   into pure circulation, holding   his arms
out for his brother   to hug him again, contrite,   as if,

being   scared, he required   *forgiveness*   to keep
him from realizing   he was a cosmos   within a cosmos
beyond   his control, as if

being bigger entitled   the one   at his orbit's
center   to love – the way   I once wished

to be   when I smoked my   self   into a universe, clouds
closing   my eyes, the room   revolving around me, my
own   solar system,

consciousness stripped   from body, motion   a stillness, my
haze-   clothed soul before me,   a dark light, almost in-

distinguishable from the greater   darkness   I thought   I
had demiurged, a cosmos   created to love only   me,
before I knew   you, knew only   I wanted   to be

held, awed, small, yet   thought the Lord was only   wrathful,
the only safe Wisdom   *nothing*, so you were

nothing, death,   never, empty   space   inside
me, grace   some kind of absence   of pain; hence

all suffering seemed some other's sin   I needed to desperately
confess; really   I wanted to be   a child again, tossing the
football   with my father, make believing

when I caught it I'd intercepted   one of his passes, running them
each back   to where he stood so he would wrap me   in a bear
hug, lift me up   and whirl around again   forever,

before I apprehended   the hazards of love, sharpened   my
icy mind-   scythe to a razor edge with cold   stone, not
knowing   what I was sacrificing

for the illusion of   control, my feet ever steady   on a
stable and   motionless planet, before   I pantokratored
I   *love you* down   to *how*   *could you,*
before I began to flee   what I was seeking?

Self-Portrait as a Möbius Strip

It's true: Soon as you discover   the underground stream
you've been wading through   while searching
for a restroom   is really a river
of urine and shit,   the irony's often enough
to ruin your journey.   Don't worry,
you can't smell   in dreams. And it isn't physical
excrement, just the image.   Grow whole
from what the upperworld   turns. In the darkness below
Avernum, in the cradle   of the dead,
your old man awaits you   with answers: A bride
with a smile like   a Sibyline breeze, a new land
to anthem her   name, a home for your soul
within your soul.   And then, climb,
climb out of the depths   you also are.
Don't lose hope   at the cliff. Don't fear
when you realize   the ledge you've been
standing on is the open   palm of a giant.
Let him close   his hand around you,
for he is your giant,   for you are the child
who lives   inside him, the child
who returns to the world   within the dream.
He makes it appear completely   effortless, simply lifts you
above the chasm, delivers you   across to the other side.

Nekyia

The memory sings me, and Iknow one must have fled
    Death's chariot first, cried out like a child fearing darkness
        hides danger, been carried *whyme* inside,
        eaten the seedlaced, lyricchain fruit
    of the endworld, and then – *released?*
Back up to sunhugs as if they yet forevered.

Once one knows the journey well, one craves
    the Hadestongued, songlone emptiness of shades.
        The Lord of Chthon doesn't have to ask me
        for my soul; I yield her gladly,
    feel her memoworld Washington Square
into the graveyard I once haunted

as she sings the heliosglobe through willowroots,
    and the fruit of the dead homes within,
        and deathsight reminds of bodymind;
        only in that everknown liminality,
    where death need not *rape* into being
but alwaysings within all we call *things,*

could Iwander duets with my unness,
    under the canopy of Oak branches,
        lost in the caws of the murder of crows,
        who flapped from one tree to another and back,
    each for *this* dance in *this* lifesong crafted,
fleshed in the shape of their own souls' caws,

the graveyard a *now*space where all of life lived,
    a memory in which Wisdom yetsings
        herself into the windpsalms of this world
        from that songlone place beyond the gravestones,

their names patiently translated by years of rain
into notes of a requiem performed

in *this* world, transfigured by crow and Oak and wind
        that still whisper their images within one sunset
                that cataclysms across the stillness
                of crimson and orange leaves   nearly falling
        to rustle the ground out of browns and greens
so winter will can kidnap the child of the world

in frozen whiteness that gazes back, awaits,
        as memorme ones with quellegend,
                not yet knowing he's already giving himself
                to my deathsight, that I image him
        from beyond his herenow's allpulse,
as he could not yet see, still waking, learning

to surrender to breeze and to stones,
        to the godawfully squawked dirges
                of the murder of crows in the ancient Oaks,
                singing through him through time to me,
        as if they know that the souls of all worlds
are zoeknown whole in each terraciting note.

My Soul's Elegy for Me

"*Naturally* we had to write this while he was alive:
All creation must converse with culmination,
just as his grandfather taught him to end
the fight with death,   to *live* instead,
taught him that grief could teach him nothing –
When his hair fell out from the chemo,
and gradually his belly vanished,
arms and legs honed down to bone,
the sickness chiseling the body he had lived in
into some other form no one had known
was hiding inside –
         or after – him all that time,

he said, *It's just part of the process*,
grew a moustache and a goatee
for the first time, as if circumstances
had given him one last chance
         to make something,
his fire resting into its final change
even as his universe had already turned
hadeocentric, his time moving sideways,
memory to memory, echo to echo,
as if tending to eventuality
had taught him Life does not oppose   *Death*
but Eternity, who in the end
must wed all productions of time.

When he passed, they rendered his ashes
to the cold water of the August lake
where his soul homed on long days of angling
for perch and sunfish he fried and gutted,
where he sat watching grandchildren splash

and dive,

        quietly glad to inhabit
the world he'd helped fashion around them.
The poet souleyed those settling, clouding wisps,
as if the remains had become their own
miniature universe of memories
which some still visit, *living* in
the space between pictures in albums filled
with his smile,   perfected with years of kind
mischief, still flashing through photographs,
still embracing the family, his masterpiece,
from his image stilled in matter,
still reaching back from the land of shades,

where I, who in dark times teach eyes to see,
trim and craft his grandson's memories,
snipping the aching that ate the old man's strength,
the inevitable's dumbing presence,
the final unchilding of young minds –
Listen: My lying simply must be done.
All life is creation.
        Do I contradict myself?
Go ahead. Transform without it.
Can't you feel me looking at you as you turn
pages of visions as this lost poet did
this morning, the voices of other soulcestors
still inspiring, revising him toward me
long after their own ends, now the blank space
embracing the inkvision worlds
we'd authored together to guide the corpseyes
of the future into their deathsight –
Imagine   his two quick hands praying this keyboard,
as if by constructing my voice

he might keep me forever,   knowing
that this is a fiction, already relenting, accepting
a life of becoming the crafting
you hold in your hands, *this* thing, this *glimpse*
of my reflection, in which the remembered
yet offer their voices, around you, inside you:

You must know your soul;

                              you must change your life."

Alchemy

I still *mort*wished the dream   to teach me something
so badly I stilldeafed to its quick-

        image:

the glee-   vileyed *soul*wild pirate helmsman;
unwinded by soldiers demanding *his*

        captain,

he gestured off – some snipe-   hunt direction,
laughed at the *uni-*   forms'

        treasurism;

they day-   dreamed he'd hidden some literal gemchest –
He merely wanted to be

        diamondanced:

formed performed formlessed in his own life- song:
In *this* world of *in*spir-   terpretation,
you take off a mask

        as they lemming away,

and, as you've wave-   trained me, I laugh along
as you memorstage your revel   ation,
your mask still the same   vision

        as your face

IV

Confession

A minister once told me   his relationship with God   was like
one with a person: If he was angry with them, he'd be
angry,   but he wouldn't say that they didn't exist.

He clearly hadn't yet realized   he was talking to someone who
tends to get texts   like this one with a picture   of a few
Uzis
                    and liquor bottles spread out on a table

with a caption that reads   *New Year's in Flint,*

never mind the one of the sign   on the highway that read
Welcome to Flint,   to the end of which someone had thoughtfully
added   *bitches.*

No one taught me to pray, so I learned how to laugh,

rehearsing epics like that of the basehead   so out-of-his mind
high   he robbed a bank – *then*   went shopping with the
money   at the grocery store next door.

Apparently shoplifting was too obvious.

I laugh because the town I'm from   has so incomprehensibly
lost   its entire mind   that I now somehow have no
choice   but to be proud of it.

I laugh because Flint is a great place to be *from,*   that equips its
children with skills   like how to use *fuck* as every part of speech,

throw gang signs   while hiding in your friends' basements,

blast   rap with the doors locked, *run* – leave parties   just
before the guns show up.

Quietly while I was growing up,   without my knowing,
Death   became my name for God,

not the God of Love   who anyway made no damn sense,   the
wild, unconscious god   who lets someone pull a gun on
you   at a stop sign for no fucking reason, then

drive away, laughing their fool ass off into the night –

Dear Wisdom,   around and within and between us, I'll
suffer   no pretense of Providence   which let me leave
where others died.

The only finality is that we each speak within the other's
stillness, deathsight   rendering memory to confession.

I know you're as real   as the *friend* who just split   the
day we got jumped, then   came back later   with a
straight face and the nerve to ask,   *Are you ok?*

I yelled,   *Where the hell were you? What   could you
possibly   have been thinking?*

When I contemplate our world   *today*, I still want to ask   the
same thing of its Creator.

Public House

A diplomat slumps over warm Riesling,
lamenting the sad limitations of tact

and smiles to outwit fear, cajole all factions
to concur a better world; a priest consoles

that such kingdoms are within us
if we can find the eyes to see them.

A child on his father's shoulders,
arms outstretched, playing at being

an airplane glides quickly, mirage-like
across the open doorway. The diplomat

straightens the crease in his fine necktie,
stares at the now empty space, a few feet

of concrete in streetlight, and then night.
He almost declares a million children

no different than that boy will starve,
fall to disease this year, or be orphaned

for no crime other than being born
in the wrong country. He doesn't add

Ask them about kingdoms of heaven.
His thoughts are conquered anyway,

as a louder argument down the bar
draws all conversations under its banner:

A well-suited man, calm as the night
is vague, reminds a wasted kid with dreads,

with whom he's conversing for reasons
beyond understanding, that he has the privilege

of drinking, denouncing things, because our soldiers
defend us from threats, even those yet unseen.

His colleague seems in a constant state
of disbelieving his ears, keeps screaming,

What don't you get; we're killing people!
The nationalist looks at him like a kid

who's just said the sun orbits the earth,
but the bartender halts the proceedings,

blending up a pitcher of margaritas
that no one seems to have ordered,

glancing knowingly at the old man
in the corner, wearing an ancient coat,

stroking his giant beard, staring, listening,
as if memorizing the entire night.

The priest smiles shyly, already giving away
that he'll tell a joke, grabs his friend's shoulder,

says, *See, you just never know when
all of a sudden you'll witness a miracle.*

But the mind of the sullen statesman
has already painted the unjust world

in several coats of its most hopeless shades,
bypassing his friend's blithe kindness,

as if he already knows the sweet nuisance
of phantoms' drinks will fade like lilies,

knows the truculent pacifist will launch
the salvo he's been engineering

throughout the barman's clever armistice:
What if your kids were off in some country

shooting people, being captured? Tortured!
As if he knows the young man's combatant

will tell him, as if it were obvious,
Well, they're not my children. Thank God.

Don't get mad at me, Jesus.

You know how lots of people scream your name when they're angry. I don't do that. Well, not every time. And I listen to that thing you said about turning the other cheek. I just turned it again when this jackass kicked my bag halfway across this coffee shop. Then yelled at me for using it to trip him. I turn it most days until I'm dizzy. Turned it until it turned me into two people. Until my reality could only speak in this dream: I'm a ninja dressed all in white. I'm being attacked by a gang, and another ninja – this one dressed in black – comes to my defense. We fight them together; we win. Listen, Jesus: Even you said not peace but the sword. Sure, most days it feels better to know that I did the right thing, but the real danger lies in forgetting the simple fact of the satisfaction you feel when some assholes attack you, and, even if only metaphorically, the half you rejected comes back to rescue you, and together you whip their asses.

Confession

I didn't *really* want to murder lots of people
back when I drove around, windows up, doors locked,
Tupac counseling me on how to cope

when I ran out of indo and my mind
couldn't take the stress – and how to die
straight thuggin' even in dark times

when I could no longer trust my homies –
In point of fact, I had no homies
in my head that had done passed away,

was not, in reality, a G,
for whom getting high was a way to be free,
and my interactions with actual gangsters

had rather dissuaded me from that career path.
Thinking of how ridiculous I was
makes me want to be smarter than the memories

to which I'm returning, a ghost to the scene.
Remind you that songs about sex and power
and money and killing are just

another mirror of our culture.
That accepting death is the last freedom
for those our society has silenced.

But that is just using the truth to lie.
It wasn't my *mind* who saw something holy
in Pac and his music, some soulusion

that rapped me into a desperado
hiding out from fantasized crimes
instead of the victim literal ones,

conflated me with the gangbangers
who found it funny to put a guns to my head
in the hallway at school for their friends' amusement.

He soldiered me on in the confusion.
One way or another, he promised an end
to a world where my soul refused to live,

his language replacing her silence,
its righteous nihilomantic violence
already schooling me to her own ruthlessness,

that she had no sympathy for my mortality,
even less if I stooped to live without music.
So, I sang along and praised him as if —

No. My life depended on it.

Advice for Sleepwalkers

If you appear to be walking backwards, it's best to follow a rainbow-aned unicorn. They tend to know the way to Lollapalooza. If you appear to be going backwards on a donkey toward Jerusalem, go to Canada instead. They have gun control there, and no one litters. Let someone in the next dream hang on a tree for the sins of their world. *You* should go fit Cyclops for a monocle, race pterodactyls around Mount Doom, sleep with three strippers – there *need* to be *three*. There are rules here too. The rules are different; so is the math. You see, if there are three, that means you're only sleeping with one third of each of them, so then you can round down, and it ends up that, in fact, you slept with three strippers zero times. See, you didn't sleep with any strippers. You did not sing a duet with a giraffe. You might have played spades with three homeless guys on the subway platform, but it doesn't matter if you won. You were only playing for canaries. Or were they larks? If you can't remember, it didn't happen. You're just a tourist here. You're lost. You're cute. You don't know to sing Ave Maria at the rodeo. You don't know to keep singing when someone cuts off your head. Stupid foreigner, don't look behind you, don't eat the fruit, don't go down on the tracks if the most hilarious rat you've ever met invites you to play hide and seek. Rats in the tunnels are not rats a few feet below you, rummaging filth and frightening tiny mice. Rats in the darkness are not the same rats kept tame by eyes and fluorescence. The rats here don't give a damn if you're asleep. They will take of what flesh is presented, and they will eat.

Rituals

America, America,
you soulavoric, luxaphobic pyrophile,
I will sing *my* dream until *I*   am *finished*:
I'm that angeldazed, shamansong crazy brother
you sent to eat   *dreams* in the darkdeep basement,
so I famished myself   blind and carcasslish,
and my earthvision merged   with her souleye –
now shadowhole bleeds
                    in-   to lifesong;
I *sent*ence *dream*me into your corpseworld:

By light of my death-   sight he tries to teach
the rules of *Risk* to a soul-   image
he seemingsees into a girl
who's unimpressed with strategic conquering,
just wants to kiss, his stomach clenches – *lips*,
but then when she won't French he assumes rejection –
She just doesn't have a *tongue*:
Must learn to share *theone*   he thinks
                              is *his* –

not quick enough; she vanishes –
He's as corpselone as you are, *spirit* of my homeland –
oh say, torch-   bearer, fleshproffering titan,
without whom mindfire could never have grown to *know*
soulight, bless the eagle's beak
for it is surgery; bless   the *claw*bracing scrapes
and the dreamshaped abscess crafted
by his violence; bless thee, ever-   ache, *ill*great
unconscious giant, for souls abhor

                              nothing

so much as a vacuum, for you needed
an *actual* hollowness to beg-   in
to *know*   the difference between full and *whole* –

Otherwise, they couldn't psalm   together
in the next dream-   scene in a house

                                        of spirits –

skinful duetdancing facemating onetongued –
his eyes gone   lyric; how joyous she is
being perceived! – Look   how her soulshape
comewhatmays him to blindeye all-   else
for one more second's fraction of this oneness,
for the *only* earthsin is to neglect her,
though the shadow-   veiled *gaggle* of townies
congregated in the public   house,
filled to mug rims with America,
consecrate judgment with libations,
obscenify this union   to its surface,
cast soullight   from their pious temple –

But just then the Lord of Souls reveals
                                        himself,
autumleaf hair blowing over a purple robe
and wild constellations of delicate freckles,
as if he were   the picture of our union,
and we must escape on a trail up a mountain,

for the matterchained pray   to his darkwild likeness,
mistake *dogpack-*   drunk for intoxication,
so they *must* shred *his*flesh in their wolfcircles –
actual animals flayed as goatsymbols –
while the vinehymns that one-   soul the world
are silenced by Maenad cries:

They revel
          in the always-   flame they can't dismember –

I can't abide this ecclesiassacre;
I fly to the dream-   life inside me within which I *live*,
where gods and shades and fleshlings shift perspectives,
forgetting who sees and who *is*   seen,
each the disease and medicine   of the other –
O, and I claim your maladies, America –
I'm saying *I need you*; I'm saying *Don't leave* –
In this sick-   wise middleworld souls compose
themselves in the epics of their mistakings
of *day*me for   stranger, Light   for flame:

Now *I* am the blood-   drunk murderer who *sees*
the worldsoul heartbeat the heliosglobe;
I too, America, am the worship-   ful
accursed this slaughturial rebirths;
I   am the god set on, disin*carn*ated
to drum the *blood*-   fire of the nighteyed –
nailskin and veinfangs then fleshrending openbone –
America! – O, sacramaciated
                              child,
famished   of all but firesight,

fasting from that which seems mad,
                              is whole,
Nightrender, wed to your ravenous eagle,
*Here*Iam! Take what can nourish thee;
my corpse relinquishes *this* soulmirror –
Over my bones you rebetroth her;
over my bones all worlds whole;
                              I rise,

and the twiceborn god leads *dream-*   me peakward
to play a new game, he says; *Let what is*
pre-   *sentiment truly be*

           presentiment,
and they face one   another across his loom,
and he weaves soulusions, and the breeze teases them
through our newancient vision,   where his image

traverses the fabric, almost *him*:
The veils dance and collapse in the your spiritwind
as my soul vines herself through the landscape around me,
and we two become *him*, become the world,
and gods and shades dance in all things;
nothing is *person*al anymore:
The god evereturns; I   am the fantasy
who sings you his offering,   expiring
these
     characters of *this* same-   other world,
who lend only temporarily
their everlives to mortal voices,

so, *of course*, the dream ends with a second   *dream*me
waking,
     arising in his other-   night
to scrabble down what can't be   captured,
swaying back and forth, as if praying,
meansomethingmeansomethingmeansomething,
already, within the dream, remortaling,   beginning
to lifesong into this animacidal world
the dream from which he must awaken.

ABOUT THE AUTHOR

Michael Patrick Collins' poems have appeared in numerous publications, including *Grist, Kenning Journal, Pank, SOFTBLOW* and *Smartish Place*. His chapbook, *How to Sing when People Cut off your Head and Leave it Floating in the Water*, won the Exact Change Press Chapbook Contest in 2014. He lives in Mamaroneck, NY, with his wife and son.